SPOTLIGHT ON NATURE

BEAVER

PAMELA DELL

CREATIVE EDUCATION · CREATIVE PAPERBACKS

Published by Creative Education and Creative Paperbacks
P.O. Box 227, Mankato, Minnesota 56002
Creative Education and Creative Paperbacks are imprints of The Creative Company
www.thecreativecompany.us

Design by Blue Design, Inc.
Art direction by Graham Morgan

Images by Dreamstime/Avslt71, 15, Crystalseye, 21, Jnjhuz, 1, Karayuschij, 2–3, 29; Getty Images/Axel Heimken/picture alliance, 12, Cavan Images, 4–5, Chase Dekker Wild-Life Images, 27, Kathleen Reeder Wildlife Photography, 11, Pam Jenks / 500px, 16, Stan Tekiela Author / Naturalist / Wildlife Photographer, 23, Troy Harrison, 24; Pexels/Andrew Patrick Photo, 29, Denitsa Kireva, 9, Nathan Cima, cover, 29; Unsplash/Derek Otway, 21, Mark Ma, 29, Ng Sze En, 17, Tim Umphreys, 10; Wikimedia Commons/Allen & Ginter, 8, 10, 15, 16, 20, 22, Courtney Celley/USFWS, 28, GrandTetonNPS, 6, Skot, 18, Steve, 14

Library of Congress Cataloging-in-Publication Data
Names: Dell, Pamela author
Title: Beaver / by Pamela Dell.
Description: Mankato, Minnesota : Creative Education and Creative Paperbacks, [2026] | Series: Spotlight on nature | Includes bibliographical references and index. | Audience: Ages 10-13 | Audience: Grades 4-6 | Summary: "An immersive wildlife book for upper-elementa ry and middle-school readers, featuring a captivating beaver family narrative, stunning photography, and educational tools like infographics, a glossary, and an index. Explores species, habitats, and conservation, making it perfect for nature lovers and young conservationists"— Provided by publisher.
Identifiers: LCCN 2025020687 (print) | LCCN 2025020688 (ebook) | ISBN 9798895810828 library binding | ISBN 9798896800354 paperback | ISBN 9798895812082 ebook
Subjects: LCSH: Beavers—Juvenile literature
Classification: LCC QL737.R632 D455 2026 (print) | LCC QL737.R632 (ebook) | DDC 599.37—dc23/eng/20250728
LC record available at https://lccn.loc.gov/2025020687
LC ebook record available at https://lccn.loc.gov/2025020688

Printed in the United States

CONTENTS

MEET THE FAMILY

BEAVERS

of North America

The North American continent is a huge landmass in Earth's western hemisphere. Its largest countries are the United States, Canada, and Mexico. But 20 other independent nations are also a part of North America. As well as many diverse countries, North America also includes a wide range of climates and geography. There are snowy mountainous regions, deep forests, burning deserts, and sandy beaches. In other parts of North America lie vast prairies, grasslands, and wetlands. Animal life is abundant here, from huge elk to the tiniest of rodents and birds. Insects and plant **species** can be counted in the thousands. All over North America, in its lakes, rivers, and marshes, lives one large, hardworking mammal, the North American beaver.

Beavers build their homes, or lodges, in water. In the spring, females prepare to give birth. The birth occurs hidden away inside the lodge. After three months of **gestation**, the litter of baby beavers, called kits, is finally born.

CLOSE-UP

The Beaver Lodge

Building a lodge starts with piling branches, mud, stones, and grass in water. Beavers then hollow out a dry chamber above the waterline, with tunnels connecting it to the outside.

CHAPTER ONE

LIFE BEGINS

Beavers are found in many of the world's **temperate ecosystems**. They are divided into two species. These are the North American beaver (sometimes just called the American beaver) and the Eurasian beaver (sometimes called the European beaver). All beavers share the same basic appearance. Their chunky bodies are covered with thick brown or gray fur. They have small eyes, large, webbed hind feet, and flat, scaly tails. Eurasian beavers are generally lighter in color, longer in size, and have narrower tails. Beavers also have four sharp incisor teeth, perfect for cutting down trees and stripping bark.

North American beavers live in Canada, northern Mexico, and all of the United States except Hawaii. They are the continent's largest rodent. They grow throughout their lives, and adult beavers typically weigh 40 to 70 pounds (17–32 kilograms). Their bodies, from tip of nose to end of tail, measure 3 to 4 feet (0.9–1.2 meters) long. Male and female beavers are about the same size, but females are sometimes larger.

BEAVER MILESTONES

DAY 1

- Born fully furred, eyes only slightly open
- Incisor teeth already beginning to show
- Weight: about 1 pound (454 grams)
- Length: about 12 inches (34 cm) including tail

Beavers are vegetarians. They actively forage, or look for food, at dawn and dusk. They enjoy eating twigs, leaves, and the soft inner bark of trees and shrubs. Aspen trees are their favorite, but they also like birch, willow, and cottonwood. Sometimes they eat grasses, water plants, or parts of crops.When winter comes, foraging becomes difficult if not impossible. Then beavers eat the tree bark and other plant material they have stored in the underwater mud. The cold water acts like a refrigerator and keeps the food fresh.

A long list of wild animals considers beavers a tasty meal. Wolves are their top **predators**, but bears, cougars, and bobcats also hunt them. Even otters, foxes, and great horned owls sometimes eat beavers. When a beaver

CLOSE-UP

Teeth

Beavers have flat molars and four long, sharp front teeth called incisors—two on top and two on the bottom. They use them to cut down trees. The incisors grow constantly, but daily gnawing keeps them from getting too long.

FEATURED FAMILY

Welcome to the World

Spring is blooming. Wherever beavers are found, this is the time when their kits are born. In early May, in a lodge built close to the bank of a lazy river, a mother beaver gives birth. Her annual litters range from two kits to eight or nine. But this time the mother beaver has four babies, a typical number. The tiny kits' birth takes place in the warm, dry, living quarters of the lodge. Now it is up to both of their parents to keep them alive.

feels in danger, it slaps its big, paddle-like tail on the water. This loud noise warns other beavers and scares away threats.

A beaver lodge is like a family home. The mother, father, and their young work together to build the lodge and find food. Kits learn to swim quickly, but when they are very young, they stay mostly in the dome-shaped lodge's safe, dry living area. Their mother stays with them during the spring and summer. When the kits grow older, they start to help out around the lodge.

1 WEEK

- Skilled at swimming but not heavy enough to dive

2-3 WEEKS

- Begins eating solid food brought by parents and siblings

CLOSE-UP

Fur

Beaver fur can be light tan or almost black. Coarse, shiny "guard hairs" form the waterproof outer layer. The soft, oily undercoat traps air bubbles to keep the beaver warm.

FEATURED FAMILY

First Meal

Once the kits are cleaned up, it's time to eat. Their parents will raise the kits together, but for now, their mother is in charge. The kits' eyes are barely open, but they are well aware of their mother's presence. They cling to her, ready for their first taste of milk. Soon they will be able—and eager enough—to stand up on their hind legs to nurse. Even though they can swim soon after birth, the tiny kits stick close to their source of food and stay dry.

BEAVERS

forage for food dawn, dusk and during the night.

3-4 WEEKS

- Begins venturing outside the lodge

4 WEEKS

- Weight: 3.75-4 pounds (1.7-1.8 kg)
- Fur becomes waterproof

CLOSE-UP

Nose and Ears

Beavers have nose and ear valves that close tightly when they dive, keeping water out so they can stay underwater longer.

CHAPTER TWO

EARLY ADVENTURES

When a male and female beaver get together, they stay together for life, only seeking a new mate if one partner dies. Mating typically occurs in January or February. Every spring, females give birth to one litter per year. The entire family, known as a colony, lives together in the lodge. This group usually includes the mother, the father, that year's new kits, and those born the previous year, making the colony typically consist of two to eight members.

Beavers are shy and **territorial**, but they don't mind sharing their habitat. Many other creatures, such as frogs, mice, and even muskrats, are welcome to find shelter in their lodges. Beavers are also very industrious, which means they are always working hard, from which came the well-known phrase "busy as a beaver." When not sleeping, beavers actively forage for food and build their lodges and dams. Their ability to take down entire trees to construct strong dams is remarkable. By damming a stream of

6 WEEKS

- No longer nursing

water, beavers create ponds. In turn, these ponds create a safety zone to hide out in, giving beavers greater protection from prey.

Within their first few weeks, beaver kits begin to eat solid food. At first, other members of the colony bring food to the kits, but soon the young beavers venture out on their own for both food and play, while the rest of the family continues with its tasks. These lively and vocal youngsters splash, dive, wrestle, and even practice slapping their tails against the water. For now, no one expects the kits to contribute to the work.

(2) MONTHS

- Able to dive and stay under water longer
- Begins exploring outside the lodge

CLOSE-UP
Hands
Beavers have five-fingered hands with strong claws. They use them to dig, build, and eat food like humans eat corn on the cob.

FEATURED FAMILY

Growing Quickly

Summer is well underway. The four beaver kits have stopped nursing. But in just a few months of life, they have already gained several pounds. They are heavy enough now to dive deep into the water and stay there without popping back up. When going out to forage, the kits sometimes ride on their mother's strong, flat tail. Sometimes she carries them in her arms. In the water, they may ride on her back. This is how they learn how and where to find good food.

CLOSE-UP

Back Feet

A beaver's large, webbed back feet have five toes each, with one split toenail that acts like a comb for grooming.

FEATURED FAMILY

Give It a Try

After a playful summer, the beaver kits are gaining new skills. October has come. Their colony must prepare for the long, cold months of winter ahead. The older family members fell trees and gather food to store in their pond's muddy bottom. Imitating their elders, the kits strip bark from the many aspen trees near the banks of their home. When a fox comes lurking, one kit does as he's been taught. He slaps his tail hard against the water, scaring the fox away. The colony is safe for now.

Felling a tree is hard work, but DAM-BUILDING must go on!

8-12 WEEKS

- Mother leaves kits to rest in another nearby den
- Father watches over kits while mother is away

CLOSE-UP

Castor Sacs and Oil Glands

Castor sacs under a beaver's belly produce strong-smelling paste for scent marking and attracting mates. Beavers also waterproof their fur by combing oil from **glands** under their tails.

CHAPTER THREE

LIFE LESSONS

Beavers are built for the water. They are slow and awkward on land, but they are expert swimmers. This skill helps them avoid predators. Their ability to build lodges, bank dens, and dams makes them nature's true **engineers**. Beavers are the only species besides humans that can dramatically change their surroundings to suit their needs. These changes greatly affect the people, plants, and animals around them—sometimes for worse, but often for better. It can take a beaver less than 24 hours to build a strong, watertight dam. When the area floods, it creates a pond that provides a perfect habitat for water birds and shorebirds. Beaver dams provide drinking water for mammals and improve soil conditions for water plants. They also boost water supply to lands that desperately need it.

6 MONTHS

- Weight: 13 to 15.5 pounds (6-7 kg)
- Able to help with food storage
- Able to help build lodges and dams

Beaver lodges are like islands whose only entrances are underwater. The lodge has a small opening at its top, called a chimney, to let in air. The walls are about 1 foot thick (.33 m) and the dry floor is covered with wood shavings for bedding. Sometimes, when the water flow is too strong to build an island-type lodge, beavers build dens on the banks of streams or rivers. These large rodents constantly work, maintaining or building their homes as needed.

As the kits grow up, they learn how to forage. They become skilled at helping to build dams and the colony's lodges. They learn that a wild slap of their tail against the water will help them scare off enemies. Young beavers also watch how their parents build scent mounds within their territory. These mounds tell other animals that the territory is taken.

FEATURED FAMILY

This Is How It's Done

A year has passed. The four young beavers are no longer kits. They are no longer the youngest in their family. They are yearlings, brothers and sisters to their mother's three newborn kits. Their parents are still the bosses of the lodge. But the yearlings have greater power than the kits. Their job is to help bring the kits their first tastes of solid food. The yearlings use gestures and postures and their voices to teach their younger siblings how things work in the lodge. The yearlings are now an important and useful part of the colony.

CLOSE-UP

Tail

A beaver's flat, scaly tail is paddle-shaped, about 6–8 inches wide and 10–12 inches long. Beavers use it to steer, swim, and communicate.

2 YEARS

- Weight: 35 pounds (16 kg)
- Has mastered the art of tree felling
- Leaves home to find own territory

3 YEARS

- Begins reproducing

They're also used to communicate with family members and with possible mates.

At about two years old, young beavers are driven off by their parents. They have grown too big for the lodge. They must then search far and wide for their own territories. Once they find a location, they build their own structures and eventually start a new colony. With good fortune, the knowledge they have gained will enable them to live 10 to 15 years in the wild.

CLOSE-UP

Eyelids

Like other animals, beavers have regular eyelids. But they have a second set as well. These see-through second eyelids protect the beaver's eyes when swimming, just as people's swim goggles do. Without this pair of clear eyelids, getting around underwater would be difficult.

FEATURED FAMILY

Practice Makes Perfect

The four young beavers have turned two years old. They know how to find food for themselves. After watching and practicing their family's tree-felling techniques, they have also mastered this essential skill. They have helped build sturdy lodges and dams. But it's their third spring. A new litter of kits will soon arrive. The younger siblings, now yearlings, are still at home, too. The lodge is too small for all of them. One day these four eldest beavers get kicked out. But they are well prepared to search out new territories and find lifelong mates of their own.

Once beaver KITS come out of the lodge, they learn all about survival.

10-15 YEARS

- End of life in the wild

19 YEARS

- End of life in captivity

CHAPTER FOUR

LEAVE IT TO THE BEAVERS

Around the world, beavers are in good shape. They are not in danger of **extinction**. Today, the North American beaver population numbers about 10 to 15 million. The Eurasian beaver count is estimated at 1.5 million. On both continents, their numbers are growing. But it was not always this way. Beavers were once on the verge of being totally wiped out.

Hundreds of years ago, around 100 million beavers roamed North America. Another 1 million, at least, existed in Europe. But these big rodents were prized for their soft, thick **pelts**. In the 1700s and 1800s, the beaver fur trade exploded. Hats made from beaver fur especially became "the thing to have." North American hunters and trappers made fortunes shipping pelts to Europe, where there were fewer beavers. Other beaver species that existed back then completely disappeared. Some beaver populations of the remaining two species went extinct, too.

In the early 1900s, limits were introduced to curb beaver hunting, and efforts to reintroduce these animals into their natural habitats began.

These protective measures have allowed beaver populations to recover. Today, they are afforded considerable protection both in North America and abroad. For instance, in 2019, California became the first state to ban the sale of new beaver fur products, and restrictions on hunting, trapping, and reintroduction programs continue to help beaver populations boom.

Despite these successes, beavers still face everyday dangers. Loss of habitat and periods of food scarcity, territorial disputes that can lead to injury or infection, severe weather events (floods, droughts, harsh winters), and risks such as drowning or falling trees remain constant threats. Road accidents, collisions with motorboats, polluted waterways, and ongoing hunting and trapping further endanger them.

It's hard to overestimate the dramatic and positive effects nature's most skilled engineers have on the environment. Though beavers are sometimes considered a nuisance, their dams help reduce drought and flooding conditions. Their influence on waterways increases **biodiversity** and improves water quality. That's why organizations such as Beavers Northwest in Washington state, and others, are dedicated to finding ways for humans and beavers to coexist. Leaving beavers to do their industrious work benefits people and the planet in countless ways.

FAMILY ALBUM

SNAPSHOTS

Beavers are the second-largest rodent in the world. The only bigger rodent is the South American capybara.

Beavers are known as a keystone species because of their huge impact on the communities in which they live.

A beaver colony's typical dome-shaped **lodge** can stand as high as 6.5 feet (2 m) and be as wide as 39 feet (12 m). A family of beavers working together can build a 35-foot (11-meter) dam in just one week.

Beavers work on felling trees mostly at night. One single beaver can gnaw down a medium-sized tree in a single night.

The world's largest beaver dam, in Canada, is about .5 miles (0.8 km) long and can be seen from space.

Beavers have oversized lungs. This feature allows them to stay underwater for as long as 15 minutes at a time.

At their top speed, beavers can swim 5 miles (8 km) per hour. This is more than two times faster than the average human can swim.

Beaver **incisor** teeth are orange due to all the iron in their tooth enamel. All that iron gives them the strength to gnaw through wood.

Eurasian beavers were once common throughout Europe and Asia, from the United Kingdom to eastern Siberia in Russia. Today, 85 percent of them live in Europe.

The paste produced by beavers' **castor** sacs is thick, brown, and vanilla-scented. It is sometimes used in perfumes and as a vanilla flavoring in foods.

Beavers are protected by law in most parts of North America. They're also protected in Scotland (2019) and England (2021) but still unprotected in Wales.

WORDS to Know

biodiversity the great variety of animals, plants, and other living things found in the world

ecosystem an interconnected group of species and the physical environment they inhabit

engineer one who knows how to design and build a machine, building, or other structure

gestation the amount of time a pregnancy lasts before birth

gland an organ in an animal's body that produces useful chemical substances

extinction when an entire species of plants or animals is permanently gone from Earth

pelt the skin of an animal with fur, hair, or wool still attached to it

predator an animal that hunts other animals

species a group of living things that have shared characteristics and are able to reproduce with one another

temperate a climate or region that has a mild climate

territorial when an animal actively defends or guards an area it claims as its own

LEARN MORE

Books

Gop, Betsy Cushing. *What Goes on Inside a Beaver Pond*. Minneapolis, MN: Storey Publishing, LLC, 2023.

Klatte, Kathleen A. *Beavers: A Wetlands Keystone Species*. New York: Rosen Publishing, 2025.

Tracy, Kristen. *When Beavers Flew: An Incredible True Story of Rescue and Relocation*. New York: Random House Studio, 2024.

Websites

"American Beaver." University of Michigan BioKids.

https://www.biokids.umich.edu/critters/Castor_canadensis/

"Beaver." Encyclopedia Britannica Kids.

https://kids.britannica.com/kids/article/beaver/352837

"Beaver." National Geographic Kids.

https://kids.nationalgeographic.com/animals/mammals/facts/beaver

Documentaries

Koenigsberg, Sarah, dir., cinematographer. "*The Beaver Believers*." Walla Walla, WA: Tensegrity Productions, 2019.

Low, Stephen, dir. "*Beavers: The Biggest Dam Movie You Ever Saw*." Chatsworth, CA: Image Entertainment, Inc., 2005.

Note: Every effort has been made to ensure that any websites listed above were active at the time of publication. However, because of the nature of the Internet, it is impossible to guarantee that these sites will remain active indefinitely or that their contents will not be altered.

Visit

HOVEY LAKE FISH & WILDLIFE AREA

Spot beavers in the wild by quietly paddling a boat around some of the area lakes' nooks and crannies.

8401 State Road 69 South
Mount Vernon, IN 47620

LINCOLN PARK ZOO

See beavers in a natural habitat at the zoo's Prizker Family Children's Zoo.

2400 N. Cannon Drive
Chicago, IL 60614

OREGON ZOO

Look for beavers busily at work in the Cascade Stream and Pond habitat in the Great Northwest section of the zoo.

4001 SW Canyon Rd.
Portland, OR 97221

SMITHSONIAN'S NATIONAL ZOO & CONSERVATION BIOLOGY INSTITUTE

Meet happy couple Juniper and Aspen at the zoo's American Trail exhibit.

3001 Connecticut Ave. NW
Washington, DC 20008

INDEX